Revolting Poems
to make you Squirm

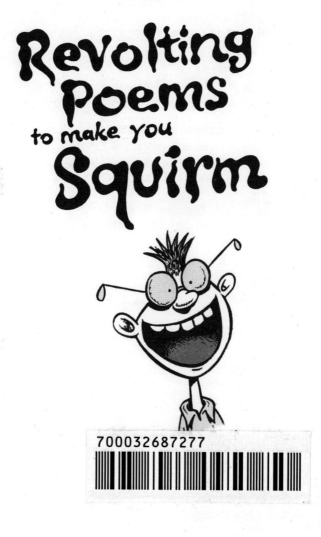

Look out for other books by Susie Gibbs:

Revolting Poems to make you Squirm

Collected by
Susie Gibbs

Illustrated by
Martin Chatterton

OXFORD
UNIVERSITY PRESS

OXFORD
UNIVERSITY PRESS

Great Clarendon Street, Oxford OX2 6DP

Oxford University Press is a department of the University of Oxford.
It furthers the University's objective of excellence in research, scholarship,
and education by publishing worldwide in

Oxford   New York

Auckland   Cape Town   Dar es Salaam   Hong Kong   Karachi
Kuala Lumpur   Madrid   Melbourne   Mexico City   Nairobi
New Delhi   Shanghai   Taipei   Toronto

With offices in

Argentina   Austria   Brazil   Chile   Czech Republic   France   Greece
Guatemala   Hungary   Italy   Japan   Poland   Portugal   Singapore
So~~uth Korea~~   ~~Switzerland~~   ~~Thailand~~   ~~Turkey~~   ~~Ukraine~~   am

Contents

Bad Habits

Don't pick your nose,
it isn't polite
and God didn't give us nails
to bite.

Don't scratch your bum.
Don't slurp your tea.
I want you to grow up
and be like me.

Sometimes Mum
makes me mad.
Why can't I grow up
and be like Dad?

Roger Stevens

Pond Vampire

I am leech

I reach
every inch of the pond
vacuum blood
suck life
from whatever moves
I can eat worms whole

but

soft bodies are
what I love most
some flesh to cling on to
some flesh to shrink small
while my corpulent length
swells and swells

I slither

from under stones
dense curtains of plants
and move
looping the loop
till I spot a fat morsel
and strike

Can you

hear their weak whimpers
their small helpless screams
as I lock them
in watery depths?
There's no shaking me off
I am Parasite Number One

I am leech

Patricia Leighton

Green

How ghastly is
the colour green.
A colour sick.
A colour mean.

Think of cabbage.
Stink of sprouts.
Grotty teeth.
Snotty snouts.

Stagnant water
deep and rank.
Slime-mossed walls,
dark and dank.

Think of foul and
furry mould
creeping over
food grown old.

Spinach slop with
gravy on it
really makes me
want to vomit.

Bilious lettuce.
Runner beans.
Don't ask me to
eat my greens!

Ann Bonner

School Dinners

Scab and matter custard,
Snot and bogey pie,
Dead dog's giblets,
And squashed cat's eye.
Spread it on your Hovis—
Spread it good and thick,
Wash it all down
With a cup of cold sick.

Anon.

What Class Four Fear the Most

We wish our teacher
Would not push
His pencil in his ear.

Not the sharp bit
But the blunt bit
It's the moment we all fear.

He wiggles it
He jiggles it
Turns it round and round.

Then pulls it out
With a squidgy slurp
And looks at what he's found.

Sometimes it's runny
Like golden honey
Dripping down his tie.

Or brown as coffee
Like sticky toffee
Crusty like a pie.

First he sniffs it
Then he licks it
Wipes it on his sleeve.

Then uses it
To mark our sums
It makes our stomachs heave.

David Harmer

Picking

Spots
Toes
Scabs
Nose
Picking's all the rage.
Just when no one's looking
Is a skill that comes with age.

Daphne Kitching

Worm Purée

Worm purée, oh hooray!
You're the dish that makes my day.
Sing a merry roundelay.
Worm purée, hooray!

Worm purée, I must say,
you're divine in every way.
Hot or cold, fresh or old,
I'm your devotee.

Worm purée, oh hooray!
You're the dish that makes my day.
Sing a merry roundelay.
Worm purée, hooray!

Worms with rice, oh so nice,
every forkful, every slice.
When I chew bits of you,
I'm in paradise.

Worm purée, oh hooray!
You're the dish that makes my day.
Sing a merry roundelay.
Worm purée, hooray!

Worms with cheese, mashed with peas,
you are guaranteed to please.
Every bite is delight,
and slides down with ease.

Worm purée, oh hooray!
You're the dish that makes my day.
Sing a merry roundelay.
Worm purée, hooray!

Worm purée, pink and grey,
you're a heavenly entrée.
Just one spoon makes me swoon,
worm purée, hooray!

Worm purée, oh hooray!
You're the dish that makes my day.
Sing a merry roundelay.
Worm purée, hooray!

Jack Prelutsky

Was it You, Grandad?

Grandad, did you give a burp?
You know, before you gave that slurp
And sucked the soup up from your spoon,
Then sprayed it all on Auntie June?
I think it *might* have been before
Uncle Jim came through the door—
You hit him nicely as you spoke
With a piece of bread that had made you choke.
Throat better now? It is? You're sure?
The tablecloth has stains galore!
Of course—*please* dab it on your chin
(Mum's serviettes ARE rather thin).
How lucky that you have a beard—
You'll not miss out, as I had feared:
With all the bits of food it traps,
You've got a *week's supply* of scraps!
If you miss your mouth and can't aim straighter,
Just take things home—and eat them later.

But forgive me if I ask once more—
Did you burp? No? Are you *sure . . . ?*

Gosh.

Then it *must* have been me . . . !

Trevor Harvey

Thunderbox

'But what *is* the thunderbox, Grandad?'
He just smiled and wouldn't say.
I couldn't help being curious
Because after breakfast each day
He'd push back his chair and announce,
'Well, it's me for the thunderbox.'
And he'd potter off across the yard
Past the sunflowers and hollyhocks.
'Well, can I come with you, Grandad?
It sounds an exciting place.'
'Afraid not,' he laughed—and Gran's there too
Trying hard to keep a straight face.
In a few days I'd worked it out:
He was off to the outside loo.
They live in a little old cottage
And their toilet's old-fashioned too.
'But why do you call it that funny name?'
Laughs now unlimited.
Gran said, 'You can surely work that out.'
And, of course, in a bit, I did.

Eric Finney

James and the Giant Spot

James once had a spot,
So what? I hear you say,
But this spot was enormous
And wouldn't go away.

'Leave alone! Don't touch it!'
Was what his mother said;
'Don't even try to squeeze it yet,
It hasn't got a head!'

But the spot just kept on growing,
It was like an extra limb;
James wondered, had he got a spot
Or had a spot got him?

He went to see the doctor
Who jumped up in surprise;
He'd seen and dealt with spots before
But never one this size!

The chemist thought that ointment might
Eradicate the spot;
He got out twenty-seven tubs
And handed James the lot.

But James's spot kept growing,
Oh, how his mother cried;
The spot grew so gigantic
James had to sleep outside.

The spot attracted interest
And drew the TV crews;
James and spot (or spot and James)
Both made the evening news.

People came with cameras
To get a family shot:
Wife and kids all standing
In front of James's spot.

Hollywood came with chequebooks;
They thought it might be groovy
To make a multi-million dollar
Film called 'Spot—the movie!'

The spot grew so colossal
That spacemen called to base:
'Houston—we have spotted it
From way out here in space.'

Mountaineers equipped themselves
With helmets, ropes—the lot—
And joined the queue to climb up to
The peak of James's spot.

Then, one night, things felt funny,
Poor James, he feared the worst;
The spot seemed kind of runny—
And suddenly—it burst!

Chunks of gunk flew skywards
At twice the speed of sound;
They reached Earth's upper atmosphere
And orbited around.

Astronomers by their telescopes,
Staring through the void,
Saw the core, and gave a roar
'We've spotted an asteroid!'

So now, with all the planets,
And stars, all white and hot,
Twinkling there, in the cold night air
Are bits of James's spot.

As for James, he's had his fame,
He showers every day
And soaps, and scrubs, and washes
To keep those spots at bay.

Martin Brown

Urrgh!

The Bogey Man

Burrowing, burrowing,
Deeper and deeper,
A frown on his forehead
As onward he goes.
Then, finally, smiling—
He's found what he's after:
It's horrible watching
My dad pick his nose.

Marcus Parry

The Scab
(for Jess, Lockie, and Jo)

I've never seen one like it.
I'd have you understand
The scab on Daddy's poorly leg
Was bigger than my hand.

Gargantuan, humungous,
A mighty king-sized slab,
And, if you didn't get a look,
You haven't seen a scab.

World's Biggest Scab

Children showed him knee-scabs
But they could not compete.
One glance at Dad's monstrosity
And they'd admit defeat.

Grown men begged to see it.
They gasped and turned quite pale
And needed something strong to drink
Before they told the tale.

The scab became as famous
As any scab could get.
Everywhere he went they asked him,
Has it come off yet?

That scab it proved a stayer.
The twenty-second day
It loosened at the edges, then
Last night it came away.

No blood and nothing nasty.
It's healed. And all that Dad
Has got to show is dark pink skin.
He's looking rather sad.

Wendy Cope

Something to Aim For

Everyone I know has thrown up,
even the Queen must sometimes spew,
but though we've all done Farmhouse Soup,
I like to be sick in a single hue.

I did a brilliant purple once
on the back seat of our car
after a heavy Ribena session,
and a road too twisty by far.

And once on a cross-channel ferry
I chucked up orange as well—
a carrot and coriander special
brought on by the heavy swell.

I did a mushy pea green sick
on my best friend's kitchen floor
and an amazing tomato and red pepper job
that ran down our bathroom door.

I've puked up yellow and I've puked in pink
but up to now I've never spewed blue.
The bringing up is easy,
any country drive will do,
but what should I eat, that's the problem—
or should I just cheat and drink
ink?

Trevor Parsons

Bogeyman School Rules

1. Do speak with your mouth full.

2. If you find interesting earwax, share it.

3. Sneeze over others whenever possible.

4. Pick your teeth at the table for five minutes after every meal.

5. Be generous with your dandruff.

6. Sniff your armpits regularly—Year 6 and above may inhale.

7. All itches are to be scratched in public.

8. Always look in the hankie after you have blown!

Sue Cowling

To My Bubble Gum

Farewell, O piece of bubble gum,
we were together a whole week
but now you are no more.

I got you on Monday,
bursting with flavour and promise
you were raring to go,
couldn't get enough of my chewing,
we limbered up.

Tuesday was our great day,
out of my pocket at playtimes
we impressed everyone
with our biggest ever
record-breaking bubble.
You even survived the explosion
onto my face
once I'd picked your bits off.

Wednesday you came off my chair
with a bit of paint attached
but were still fresh and pliable,
once I'd warmed you up in my mouth.

By Thursday you had tired,
not quite so keen,
taking on a grey pallor
you became stiff and unwilling.

Then this morning, Friday,
as I picked you off the bedside
rigor mortis had set in.
Try as I might
you were not to be revived.

And so goodbye
once chewy friend.
It was great while you lasted.

Jane Saddler

Here Lie the Bones

Here lie the bones of Horace Sands
who, when his mum said, 'Wash your hands!'
before a meal or after pees,
refused, and so a vile disease,
instead of being washed away,
just grew on fingers, till the day
it leapt from fingers into mouth,
skipped over teeth and headed south,
past throat and gullet into tum,
from where that fierce bacterium
to every limb and organ spread—
and hence young Horace Sands lies dead.

Peter Bently

Black Socks

Black socks, they never get dirty,
The longer you wear them the stronger they get.
Sometimes I think I should wash them,
But something inside me keeps saying,
'Not yet, not yet, not yet, not yet, not yet.'

Anon.

Crunch

There's a snail in my *house.*

I've seen trails in the morning—all over the walls in
a crazy gleaming pattern only visible from a certain
angle and
slime right across my carpet.

What's it doing in my *house?*

Snails live in the garden. They eat plants—
what is this snail eating in my *house?*

Maybe it's a slug?
Would that revolting slime look any different?
I don't care which it is.
I don't like snails *or* slugs.
I don't like them in my *house.*

I don't like their sticky-up alien eyes.
I don't like their squishy squashy bodies.
I don't like their shiny slimy trails.

But what I *really don't like* is getting up in the night
for a drink of water and going to the bathroom and
not bothering to put on my slippers and—

Crunch
Yup. Definitely a snail.

Madeleine Bingham

Blowing Your Own Trumpet

Little ones, big ones
Snorting like a pig ones
Short ones, long ones
Smelly welly strong ones
Deadly silent ones
Loud and violent ones
Eggy ones, runny ones
Musical and funny ones
Bubble in the bath ones
Those that make you laugh ones

All these noises, everyone's got 'em
Everybody's got a musical bottom
Everybody's got a musical bottom

Careful what you do ones
Nearly follow through ones
Those you have to push ones
Those that make you blush ones
Wet ones, dry ones
Low ones, high ones
Tears in your eye ones
Fast ones, sloooowwww ones
Five rooms in one go ones
Little squeaky mum ones
Machine gun bum ones

All these noises, everyone's got 'em
Everybody's got a musical bottom
Everybody's got a musical bottom

Squashy ones, squelchy ones
Big beefy belchy ones
Rhythmic beaty ones
Mighty, meaty ones,
Central heated ones
Rusty hinge door ones
Bounce across the floor ones
Gushy mushy peas ones
Those you have to squeeze ones
Those that shake your knees ones
Brussels sprouts and beans ones
Total quarantine ones
Make your trousers steam ones

All these noises, everyone's got 'em
Everybody's got a musical bottom
Everybody's got a musical bottom

HEE HEE HEE!

Morning-after-curry-ones . . .
To the toilet hurry ones
Surprising and unplanned ones
Just like a brass band ones
Going . . . down . . . balloooooon . . . ones
Blast off to the moon ones
Double trouble trembly ones
Middle of assembly ones
Environment unfriendly ones
Foghorn warning ones
Global warming ones

All these noises, everyone's got 'em
Everybody's got a musical bottom
Everybody's got a musical bottom

Icky ones, sticky ones
Got lost in your knicker ones
Whirlwind up your skirt ones
Cyclone in your shirt ones
Every type of noise ones
Girls' ones and boys' ones
Blow holes in your pants ones
Fertilize the plants ones

POP POP

There's no chance, there's no stopping
The flurp and the parp of fizzy whizz popping
All these noises, everyone's got 'em
Everybody's got a musical bottom
Everybody's got a musical bottom

Paul Cookson

Waiter, Waiter . . .

Customer: Waiter, waiter! There's a toe in my soup!

Waiter: Oh, lucky old you, sir. Can I have a look?
If it's got a verruca, it belongs to our cook.
He should quit 'cos his bits all drop off!

Customer: Waiter, waiter! There's a nose in my stew!

Waiter: Oops, so there is, sir. Did you give it a chew?
Cook sneezed in the gravy and off the
thing blew!
It's the pits, but his bits all drop off!

Customer: Waiter, waiter! What's that on the tray?

Waiter: It looks like a thumb, sir. It's dish of the day.
Cook might need a hand for his finger buffet.
He wears mitts but his bits still drop off!

Customer: Waiter, waiter! This steak's really rotten!

Waiter: Hold everything, sir, cook's just lost
his bottom . . .

Maureen Haselhurst

Disgusting

At the boarding house where I live
Things are getting very old.
Long grey hairs in the butter,
And the cheese is green with mould,
When the dog died we had sausage,
When the cat died, catnip tea.
When the landlord died I left it;
Spare ribs are too much for me.

Anon.

A User's Guide to the Cowpat

Dry them out and hang them
in rows up in your room.
The phosphorescent glow from them
will brighten up the gloom.

One can make a nice, cheap frisbee
or a big, brown picnic plate,
or bowl it like a hula hoop
then sling it at your mate.

They will make delightful face packs,
when moistened to a gloop
and if you're starving on the prairie
they make thick, nutritious soup.

Try them out as headgear
with a feather stuck on top
or mix them up with water,
then paddle in the slop.

You can use them as a maggot farm
or as snowshoes in a storm.
You can light a fire with them
(it's smelly, but it's warm).

I could carry on forever
but I mustn't be a bore.
Take this one as a present,
it will do to wedge the door.

Marian Swinger

Aaaaargh!

My aunty folds my face up,
Squeezes it like a concertina
Between her bony hands.
Then puckers up her mouth
into a wet doughnut—
Comeherecomeherecomehere
She says. Though I'm already there
And I can't get away.
Comeherecomeherecomehere
And I see it—
A slow-mo doughnut moving
Unstoppable through the air.
And I know, I just know,
That when it lands,
This killer kiss
Will be A WET ONE.

Jan Dean

Hang Dog

DRIPPY

DROOBILY,

DROOLY

DOOBILY,

SLIPPERY

SLUPPERY,

BLIBBERY

BLUBBERY,

DOG

SALIVA!

Tim Pointon

The Things That Get Caught in Our Teacher's Beard

It's sticky, it's slimy,
disgusting and weird,
the things that get caught in our teacher's beard.

Beans and spaghetti
caught heading south,
soggy rice crispies
that missed his mouth.

It's sticky, it's slimy,
disgusting and weird,
the things that get caught in our teacher's beard.

Old nail clippings
chewed from his toes,
bits of green stuff
blown from his nose.

It's sticky, it's slimy,
disgusting and weird,
the things that get caught in our teacher's beard.

Tomato sauce that drips from his chips,
froth from the coffee he noisily sips,
apple cores and orange pips,
pieces of chalk and paper clips.

It's sticky, it's slimy,
disgusting and weird,
the things that get caught in our teacher's beard.

Damian Harvey

It Came from the Plughole

I was just setting about
the washing-up when
out from the plughole squirmed
a greasy, snaky grey thing
all shiny with drain slime.
It kept coming and coming,
coiling itself up in the sink
and looking at me with
wicked little black eyes.

'Mum!' I screamed, getting
my wits together,
'guess what's squirming out
from the plughole. A greasy,
snaky grey thing all shiny
with drain slime. It keeps
coming and coming and it's
looking at me and the sink's
nearly full of it.'

Mum came and took a look
and said calmly, 'Oh yes,
it's one of those greasy,
snaky grey things all shiny
with drain slime that sometimes
squirm out of plugholes and
look at you with wicked
little black eyes. It'll go
back down again; look, it's
already started. Soon you'll
be able to get on with
the washing-up.'

Eric Finney

I'm Going to the Garden to Eat Worms

Nobody likes me, everybody hates me,
I'm going to the garden to eat worms.
Long, thin, slimy ones, short, fat fuzzy ones,
Gooey, gooey, gooey, gooey worms.

The long, thin, slimy ones slip down easily,
The short, fat, fuzzy ones stick,
Nobody likes me, everybody hates me,
I'm going to the garden to be sick.

You cut off the heads, and suck out the juice,
And throw the skins away.
Nobody knows how I survive
On a hundred worms a day.

Anon.

It's Such a Shock

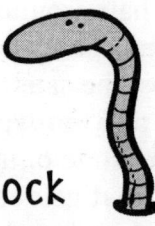

It's such a shock, I almost screech,
When I find a worm inside my peach!
But then, what really makes me blue,
Is to find a worm who's bit in two!

William Cole

The Meal That Walked

We sat at the table without a care
Until, that is, Dad found a hair
Wrapped around a single bean
And lunch ended up like a horror movie scene
As he twisted that hair around his fork
And gradually his meal began to walk.
The eggs, the chips, the sausages and
Tomatoes were all tied to that strand
Of long blond hair. None of us could even guess
As to the owner of that golden tress.
It wasn't Mum, her hair is red
And Dad is bald—not a hair on his head.
My hair is short and my sister's is too
Unless she'd stuck dozens together with glue.
And still Dad went on tug, tug, tugging
Until he found that he was lugging
All of our dinners across the room.
Mum cried, 'Go and fetch a broom
And sweep this horror off the floor
While I go and cook some more.'
But no one wanted to eat that night.
We'd somehow lost our appetite.

John Coldwell

I Wouldn't Eat THAT

Black pudding? You ask me, do I want a slice?
But I know what it's made from, it doesn't sound nice ...

So I wouldn't eat THAT,
I just COULDN'T eat THAT.

See that wobbly wet blanket you tell me is tripe—
What? You ate it in your day? You do what you like,

But I wouldn't eat that,
Really COULDN'T eat THAT.

Pig trotters, sweetbreads, brawn, and sheep's head—
Call it offal? It sounds it. No, you go ahead

Cos I wouldn't eat that ...
Yuck! I COULDN'T eat THAT.

You say chips tasted best when they cooked them in
    dripping.
If I come round for tea that's one meal I'll be skipping.

All that lard, all that fat,
Sorry—WOULDN'T eat THAT.

No, I wouldn't
Just wouldn't
Just COULDN'T
Eat THAT.

John Calvert

Pooem

There it was,
On the pavement,
Right outside the joke shop:
A plastic plop;
A trick turd;
A decoy dump;
A latex log;
A man-made moey;
A joke jobbie;
A bogus botty bomb;
Fake faeces;
Sham poo;
Pseudo doo-doo.
How obvious!
So I picked it up.
Oh.

Andy Seed

Gas Attack

My cat has halitosis,
(a top vet's diagnosis).
No matter what the dish is
it's always rotten fishes.

He's much too old to hunt now;
only gives a curt miaow.

Less tooth and claw
with gummy maw
he b r e a t h e s the mice to death.

John C. Desmond

Nasty Pets

Deep deep down
where nobody goes,
in teachers' shoes
between their toes,

You'll find blue beetles
and a worm,
with two fat fleas
which like to squirm.

You'll find a maggot
and a snail,
gobbling bits
of old toenail.

You'll find all these,
sucking sweet,
for teachers never
wash their feet.

Andrew Collett

Here Lies the Body

Here lies the body
Of Mary Rose
She ate the gunge
Between her toes.

John Kitching

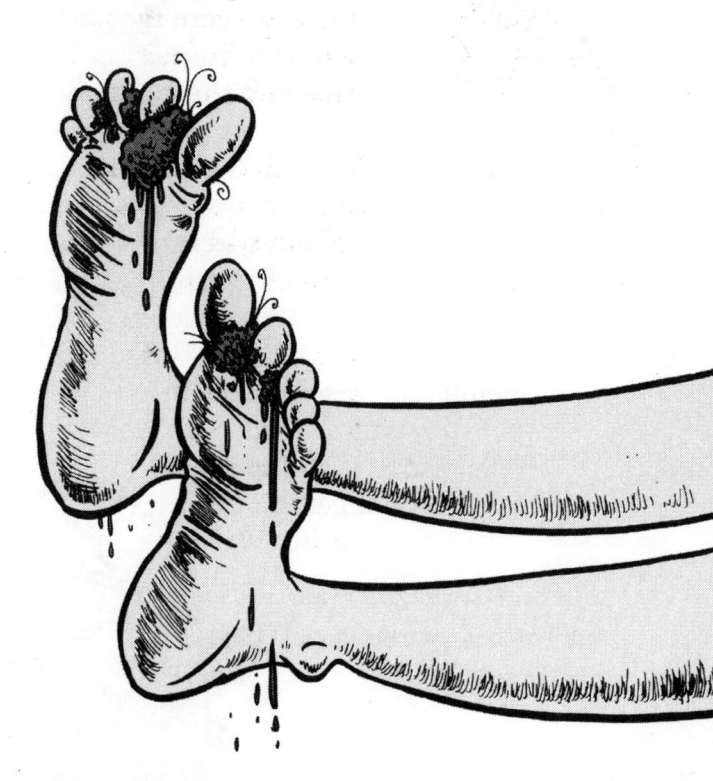

Willie's Wart

Willie had a stubborn wart
upon his middle toe.
Regardless, though, of what he tried
the wart refused to go.

So Willie went and visited
his family foot physician,
who instantly agreed
it was a stubborn wart condition.

The doctor tried to squeeze the wart.
He tried to twist and turn it.
He tried to scrape and shave the wart.
He tried to boil and burn it.

He poked it with a pair of tongs.
He pulled it with his tweezers.
He held it under heat lamps,
and he crammed it into freezers.

Regrettably these treatments
were of very little use.
He looked at it and sputtered,
'Ach! I cannot get it loose!'

'I'll have to get some bigger tools
to help me to dissect it.
I'll need to pound and pummel it,
bombard it and inject it.'

He whacked it with a hammer,
and he yanked it with a wrench.
He seared it with a welding torch
despite the nasty stench.

He drilled it with a power drill.
He wrestled it with pliers.
He zapped it with a million volts
from large electric wires.

He blasted it with gamma rays,
besieged it with corrosives,
assaulted it with dynamite
and nuclear explosives.

He hit the wart with everything,
but when the smoke had cleared,
poor Willie's stubborn wart remained,
and Willie'd disappeared.

Linda Knaus and Kenn Nesbitt

We Can Never Go Back to the Fair Again

We can never go back to the fair again
since my brother was sick on the chair-o-plane.
It flew like a whirlwind of smelly snow
onto the heads of the people below,
then it pebble-dashed innocent passers-by
and spattered the man on the coconut shy.
It landed like sludge on the waltzer where,
though people ducked it got stuck in their hair.
When the ride stopped, we leapt off and ran,
hotly pursued by the chair-o-plane man,
who roared like a lion, and puffed like a train.
No, we'll never go back to the fair again.

Marian Swinger

The Dung Beetle

What fun to be a dung beetle
rolling balls of dung;
so soft and slightly pungent
in the heat of the midday sun.

When other creatures hide away,
or in the shade go flopping,
I race around excitedly
and try to find a dropping.

Elephant poop is best, of course;
it makes the finest spheres;
especially when it's steaming hot,
I dive in up to my ears.

I dig some out and roll it up,
I'm careful not to waste it;
sometimes a bit gets in my mouth,
you really ought to taste it.

Uphill it's a struggle to push it home,
But downhill is OK.
I just grab hold and cling on tight
And wheeeee! I'm on my way.

Oh, such fun to be a dung beetle
rolling balls of dung;
so soft and slightly pungent
in the heat of the midday sun.

Mike Jubb

Henry Wells and the Silent Horror

There is a boy in our class
Whose name is Henry Wells
And Henry specializes
In producing nasty smells.
What's more, he does it *silently,*
Just how, I've not a clue:
There'd certainly be noises
If it was me or you.
So how do we know it's Henry?
He's not a boastful feller:
He doesn't tell the whole wide world,
'I am the phantom smeller.'
But we're quite sure it's Henry
Because when the odour spreads,
When that silent horror comes
That everybody dreads,
And we're all holding noses
Against a smell so beastly vile,
Henry, a boy contented,
Sits there with a smile.

Eric Finney

Out at Lunch

All morning the rain had gobbed on the windows
and going over to lunch we all got soaked so that
you could hardly see the room for the steam rising
from wet clothes and wide tins of food and what
with the dank overpowering smells and the 'flu
   coming on
my head was swimming and as we're standing in this
   mist,
in line with our trays, JJ behind me says, 'Look,
worms in blood again,' and though I knew he meant
the spaghetti I got this uneasy sensation
that the white mass was twitching but I felt so unsteady
I said nothing. It was like being inside a cloud,
not floating although my legs no longer felt sure
they were part of me and JJ's face seemed to swell
and his voice was at once far away and very loud.
'Look, cat stew, you can see bits of fur, cat spew stew,
look, green sheep droppings, and is that maggots in rice
or rice in the maggots . . .' There was no stopping him
when he'd started this game, I tell you, one time he'd
put string in his curry and insisted it was a rat's tail
long after it was funny. 'Hey, I'd like some baked bugs
   please
with mashed brains and a giant slug.' My knees
were wobbly, I took a cheese roll and an orange juice
and even they seemed too much. When we sat down
   I felt worse,
I couldn't touch the food, I stared at the table, at the
   usual
crumbs, stains, and slops, at JJ's plate opposite. Most

of all at his plate for it seemed like the beans
were squirming and one or two slid off, over the rim,
and scuttled away. It was a bit odd but I was past
  caring,
I felt like I was hanging over a huge pit, head
  spinning so
everything around was distant and dim
except for JJ's blether, now a meaningless babble
of surging waves through the blurring mist
of his left fist gripping a fork he'd just jabbed
into the mound of pale mashed potato
that looked strangely like I thought my brain felt
  inside my head
and when with a slow slither
the sausage twisted sideways and bit into his wrist
I fainted

Dave Calder

Flea Cheese

Could I have some flea cheese please.
I find a cheesy flea agrees
with me. Cheese speckled black,
bite into it and hear the crack
as fleas go pop, as fleas go squish.
It's not a vegetarian dish
being rich with blood (its main appeal).
I like a piece with every meal,
so cheap, so tasty, so nutritious.
I'll take six kilos. Mmmm, delicious.

Marian Swinger

Take a Dish of Slugs . . .

Slugs are very useful in the kitchen,
you can use them in the most exciting ways.
I like them wrapped in little lettuce parcels
and served with tangy, creamy mayonnaise.

They're also tasty fried in herbs and garlic
and delicious chopped in cottage cheese with chives,
while lightly boiled and processed in the blender
I've found they make my baby brother thrive.

A recipe I've recently discovered
is mixing them with mushrooms chopped up fine.
I stuff them into big firm beef tomatoes
and bake them very slowly—mmm! Divine!

Battered and deep fried they can't be bettered
and they're excellent, of course, with crispy chips.
In kebabs they'll have your guests all wildly guessing
and they're perfect at a barbeque for dips.

Yes, succulent soft slugs are so amazing,
so versatile and easy on the purse,
they'll soon be tops in all the TV cook shows.
(Just remember where you heard about them first.)

Patricia Leighton

Disobedient Poem

This naughty poem
Was warned by its mum and dad
To stay away from
Disgusting anthologies.
Of course it didn't listen.

Philip Waddell

Acknowledgements

Every effort has been made to trace and contact copyright holders before publication and we are grateful to all those who have granted us permission. We apologize for any inadvertent errors and will be pleased to rectify these at the earliest opportunity.

Peter Bently: 'Here Lie the Bones' copyright © Peter Bently.
Madeleine Bingham: 'Crunch' copyright © Madeleine Bingham.
Ann Bonner: 'Green' copyright © Ann Bonner.
Martin Brown: 'James and the Giant Spot' copyright © Martin Brown.
Dave Calder: 'Out at Lunch' copyright © Dave Calder.
John Calvert: 'I Wouldn't Eat THAT' copyright © John Calvert.
John Coldwell: 'The Meal that Walked' copyright © John Coldwell.
William Cole: 'It's Such a Shock' copyright © 1981 by William Cole.
First appeared in *Poem Stew*, published by HarperCollins. Reprinted by permission of Curtis Brown, Ltd.
Andrew Collett: 'Nasty Pets' copyright © Andrew Collett.
Paul Cookson: 'Blowing Your Own Trumpet' copyright © Paul Cookson.
Wendy Cope: 'The Scab' copyright © Wendy Cope.
Sue Cowling: 'Bogeyman School Rules' copyright © Sue Cowling.
Jan Dean: 'Aaaaargh!' copyright © Jan Dean.
John C. Desmond: 'Gas Attack' copyright © John C. Desmond.
Eric Finney: 'Thunderbox', 'It Came from the Plughole', and 'Henry Wells and the Silent Horror' copyright © Eric Finney.
David Harmer: 'What Class Four Fear the Most' copyright © David Harmer.
Damian Harvey: 'The Things that Get Caught in Our Teacher's Beard' copyright © Damian Harvey.
Trevor Harvey: 'Was it You, Grandad?' copyright © Trevor Harvey.
Maureen Haselhurst: 'Waiter, Waiter . . .' copyright © Maureen Haselhurst.
Mike Jubb: 'The Dung Beetle' copyright © Mike Jubb.
Daphne Kitching: 'Picking' copyright © Daphne Kitching.
John Kitching: 'Here Lies the Body' copyright © John Kitching.
Linda Knaus and Kenn Nesbitt: 'Willie's Wart' © 2004 by Linda Knaus and Kenn Nesbitt. Reprinted from *Rolling in the Aisles* (© 2004 by Meadowbrook Creations) with permission from Meadowbrook Press.
Patricia Leighton: 'Pond Vampire' and 'Take a Dish of Slugs . . .' copyright © Patricia Leighton.
Marcus Parry: 'The Bogey Man' copyright © Marcus Parry.